The Other
Little Black Book

Essentials for Men on Dating Apps

Mel W

BookLocker

Print ISBN: 978-1-958892-37-4
Ebook ISBN: 979-8-88531-704-7

Published by BookLocker.com, Inc., Trenton, Georgia.

BookLocker.com, Inc.
2024

First Edition

Library of Congress Cataloging in Publication Data
W, Mel
The Other Little Black Book: Essentials for Men on Dating Apps by Mel W
Library of Congress Control Number: 2024921515

Table of Contents

INTRODUCTION

To be honest, online dating can be tough, sometimes painful, and even soul-destroying, to say the least. There are a variety of reasons why this can happen, but the good news is that it doesn't have to be that way. If you want to improve your online dating efforts, this little black book may be just what you need.

Of the 3.2 million Australians who used dating apps last year, 73.9% were men. This explains why in a highly competitive arena, men really need to improve their chances of getting a match to at least have a place in the race. It is important for men on dating apps to put their best foot forward because people judge a book by its cover in the online jungle.

Putting your best foot forward is one of the most significant things you can do to stand out from the crowd. It's the little things like taking more time to craft an attractive profile, with well-written details and an appealing photo.

I am often called the 'Date Whisperer' and have seen it all. When reviewing dating apps, I've noticed men miss out on potential matches because of their profile content. Helping men shine online.

To help men put their best foot forward in the online dating area, I created Mel W & Co to provide a range of online resources, including articles, videos, and podcasts, to help men take their dating app game to the next level. It's about helping great guys who are overlooked by potential suitors.

This book is designed to assist you to navigate the online dating world more efficiently. It includes helpful tips on creating a profile, writing messages, and selecting the right people to connect with. It can also help you understand misreading online situations. To make it easier, there will be summarised tips at the end of each chapter.

My advice on dating apps has always been simple, in an online jungle where people judge a book by its cover, do not waste valuable opportunities to put your best foot forward,

This book will take you from being on the dating app bench to a dating app pro to increase and improve your online presence.

"If you really want to do something, you'll find a way. If you don't, you'll find an excuse."

— Jim Rohn

STEP 1: THEIR CODE AND YOUR BOUNDARIES

"To be prepared for war is one of the most effective means of preserving peace." – George Washington.

This chapter is all about preparation and awareness. Prepare yourself for combat and be aware that it is psychological warfare out there.

Technology has made people highly accessible. Like most things, it's about balance. Like the Yin and the Yang. Like sugar and salt. So, while people are highly accessible, they've also become highly disposable. This creates space for online antics.

Flirting on social media through private messaging, chatting on WhatsApp, and using dating apps can almost be compared to a virtual prison yard. Prison yard rules should define how prisoners act. They set the boundaries for what is acceptable and what is not according to their code.

The rules are loose for the social inmates you will encounter in a virtual prison yard. This chapter will help your ability to be your own virtual prison guard. It will also help you deal with social inmates, whether it be on apps, social media, in person or from afar.

To maintain your own peace inside, prepare for the war. To do that, you must understand that if you are a newbie online, you will likely encounter some crappy behaviour. If you are not new, then no doubt you have encountered some of the codes in this step.

With these codes, a person's manners and social accountability seem to have gotten lost somehow. Set your boundaries for what is acceptable and what is not according to their code. Here are a few tips to prepare you for a war where there are no real rules. Please note that some of the codes may be more applicable when your connection is in person and beyond dating apps. Still, it's important to be aware and prepared.

Their Code: Blocked. You have been blocked. All communication has abruptly ended and permanently by blocking your phone number or social media accounts and you can't access them, and you can't see any of their accounts.

Your Boundaries: Move on. If you've been blocked, try to figure out when it happened, then avoid repeating it with the next person. Albert Einstein said, 'Insanity is doing the same thing over and over again and expecting different results.'

Their Code: Breadcrumbs. Leads you on. Drops small crumbs of interest e.g. an occasional message, phone call, date plan, or social media interaction. Inconsistent contact. Usually doesn't intend to follow-through.

Your Boundaries: Fly away! You are an eagle, not a pigeon. Breadcrumbs are for pigeons! Respect yourself, spread your wings and fly away.

Their Code: Paperclipping. It is like breadcrumbing, where someone enters your life to feel good about themselves and then leaves yet again.

Your Boundaries: Close the open house! Next time you see them coming, shut the front door. You are not a cheap rental. Don't let people rent your valuable time for free. Bam! Boom!

Their Code: Ghosting. Abruptly no longer accepting or responding to phone calls, instant messages, etc. You can send messages and can see their accounts, but they don't respond or acknowledge you.

Your Boundaries: Do not disturb. If someone ghosts you, respect the dead and never disturb them again. Amen!

Their Code: Fire dooring. Your connection only works in one direction, like the fire escape doors at work. They open to evacuate down the stairs when there's an emergency, false alarm or a fire drill. However, from the outside the doors don't open to come back up.

Your Boundaries: Get into your Honda and drive away from Rhonda. Eventually, you'll feel exhausted without the Fire Department. Learn to read the room. You have two choices if you are always initiating contact... don't come back after the fire drill OR stay and ride through all the false alarms and fire drills and stop complaining.

Their Code: Cookie jarring. The person you have been seeing (without an official status) has little intention of entering a relationship with you but keeps you while seeking other partners.

Your Boundaries: Put yourself on a cookie-free diet. Reduce those calories and cut your losses. If you think this is about the chase and find it appealing, you might want to do some internal work. You deserve better so set boundaries and stick to them to protect yourself.

Their Code: Cushioning. If the current relationship fails, they always have other options to consider. This gives them a sense of security if the current relationship doesn't work out. Despite their commitment to one person, they entertain other romantic possibilities.

Your Boundaries: Use this cushion at your own risk. There is nothing soft about this cushion. This cushion has energy vampire powers. It is filled with rocks. Do not pick it up. No more needs to be said, the definition says enough.

Their Code: Freckling. UV rays stimulate melanin production in the skin, causing freckles. Think of a summer holiday, when the sun's out, the freckles are out. When the days get colder and there is less sun, these types disappear. Just like freckles appear in the summer they'll be gone by winter.

Your Boundaries: Slip, slop, slap! Slip on a shirt. Slop on dating app sunscreen. Slap on a hat to protect you from sun and pack lightly. Protect yourself when summer ends. Enjoy it knowing it may not last longer than the vacay.

Their Code: Hard balling. Their expectation of a relationship is crystal clear, whether a long-term partnership is desired or a casual one or a hook-up only. They have told you what they are prepared for or capable of.

Your Boundaries: Listen to them! Having two ears and one mouth is a positive thing, so listen more and speak less. Trying to talk to them out of what they want might be perceived as needy or that you didn't listen. When their expectations prevail, prepare yourself not to be upset.

Their Code: Haunting. An ex or former flame is still very much present on your social media. You no longer interact, but they still view all of your stories, like all of your posts, and even comment on them.

Your Boundaries: Too easy! Look good in your posts and reels. Look authentic. Look fun. Look happy. Do not write passive aggressive hints. Do not post photos of you groping others or sloppily kissing someone. Look like the guy everyone wants to be and be with.

Their Code: House planting. They treat you like a houseplant. They water you occasionally. They treat you like an object, not a person.

Your Boundaries: You are not a mushroom! Soon they'll treat you like a mushroom, keeping you in the dark and feeding you pooh so they grow! Ever smelt a mushroom farm? One of the most pungent chemicals in mushrooms is ammonia. A hot, humid environment intensifies the smell. You need to block that nose and walk.

Their Code Mosting. This is when someone goes overboard with all the fluffy compliments and romantic talk, then disappears. It's not someone complimenting and flattering; it's someone pretending to be totally smitten for some cheap interaction to feed their ego.

Your Boundaries: Lights, camera, action. Without meaning and purpose, words are cheap. Do not forget that. After many promised words are said, actions are the currency you should invest in. If they promise the world in messages or phone calls, see if they follow through. Words can be as fake as a cheap toupee without a fire hazard rating tag – dangerous as they are likely to be made of cheap, highly flammable materials.

Their Code: Pocketing. You are hidden from their friends, family or on social media. While it can be unintentional, sometimes pocketing stems from shame - figure out if it is yours or theirs.

Your Boundaries: The band aid needs to be ripped off. Bring it up. Address it. Ask them why. Regardless of the initial pain, it needs to be done. If you do not raise this issue, as in not removing the band aid, this situation will most likely get more serious. Reduce the risk of an emotional infection and remove the band aid quickly.

When you remain hidden in a dark pocket, you will eventually become insecure and toxic emotionally. It's human nature.

To help reduce inflammation and pain that is about to occur, apply R.I.C.E. – Rest to recover. Ice the temptation to beg for their return. Compartmentalise the memories and focus on your future. Elevate beyond yourself to something that makes you feel good! The person you are with should feel proud to be with you.

You know what to do - Remove the band aid and apple R.I.C.E.

Their Code: Slow Fade. It's when someone slowly ends a relationship but doesn't tell you about it. They slowly distance themselves from you. This is a way to avoid confrontation. Instead of telling you it is over, they will start to see you less, call you less, and make more excuses for not being able to see you.

Your Boundaries: Recognise the signs my brother! This is like when people slowly release air out of a balloon. Like an inflated balloon, it is full, smooth, whole and round. As the air slowly escapes, the balloon slowly becomes saggy, deflates, and eventually becomes extremely flat with crêpe like texture!

This is called slow rejection or love exhalation. It is cruel. Recognise the signs and take the necessary steps. Try talking. If they are not willing to talk, walk away!

Their Code: Submarining. They have been romantically involved with you. Something more than just friends with benefits bed buddy. Feelings and commitment were involved. Then suddenly, they ghosted you. They disappeared without notice. As if nothing had happened, then they resurfaced without an apology or explanation.

Your Boundaries: Do not engage or entertain yet again. Abort the mission! Invest in a floating vessel that is always above the water. Promote yourself to captain and take charge. Sail to another ocean and embark on a new adventure. People treat you according to how they value you.

YOUR TAKEAWAY CONTAINER

Be aware that not everyone knows how to behave. Sometimes it is not about you. It's about them.

If it looks like a duck, behaves like a duck, and quacks like a duck, then it's probably a duck and not the swan you're hoping for. Don't ignore the situation, act.

Your boundaries are more significant than their codes.

Staying is a choice and walking away is also a choice.

Choices + boundaries = freedom.

Your life is yours to create. Speak up!

Not your circus, not your monkeys but you may meet some clowns.

STEP 2: HIGH VALUE MEN

Swag is for boys. Class is for men. Drive German. Wear Italian. Drink Scotch. Kiss French.

People are magnetically attracted to high value men. What do high value men look like? They have goals with ambitions that motivate to act and succeed. Their words and actions match like a twinned couple on a Ralph Lauren fashion shoot.

These guys are the total package. Men want to be their buddy on the streets and ladies want to be their buddy between the sheets.

Why is this so? High value men know how to make women do two things!

S - Secure	O - Obtainable
Q - Quality	R - Reliable
U - Undivided	G - Genuine
I - Intelligent	A - Autonomous
R - Rakish	S - Self
T - Taste	M - Maker

This may inspire you to do a general maintenance scan and give you some ideas. This step is looking at all your activities, assessing your life accounts, cleaning up and tidying up your inner being to lead you to a more productive online presence as you are feeling good about your high value life.

Let's see what high value men offer and how you can reach full access and membership to the club.

S is for SECURE.

If you are a high value man then you are secure in your own skin with a healthy level of self-worth, self-esteem, and practice self-care. Even as a joke, they don't engage in self-deprecation dialogue about themselves. High value men don't belittle themselves or give others the opportunity.

Your takeaway from this: Know your worth. If you don't, it's time to invest in yourself.

Take the time to listen to podcasts or YouTube clips. Success Chasers on YouTube is a great start. If you start making self-deprecating jokes about yourself in front of women, you want to impress - stop yourself. Why offer your shortcomings on a platter?

Q is for QUALITY.

High value men work to maintain balance in life's four domains - work, physical, social, and spiritual. Actions speak volumes. One thing a quality man will often do is not buy into quantity.

Your takeaway from this: Balance. Get the recipe right. Counteract the salty and sour with sweet. Schedule some routine time for yourself and commit to it.

It could be every Sunday night or Monday morning. Doesn't matter - just start.

Week 1 - Under the domains of work, physical, social and spiritual, write a list of what your strengths are and where you want to improve.

For example, under work, take a course, watch YouTube videos on how to increase your skills with a certain program, then practice it.

Under physical, start meal prep for a balanced diet. Swim twice a week before or after work. Establish a sleep schedule.

Under social, consider joining a club that interests you, such as running clubs, meetup groups, team sports clubs, sailing clubs even book clubs. Just get out there.

Under spiritual, become aware and reconnect with your source by walking barefoot on the grass. Start a writing down what you are grateful for. Basically, find three things you are grateful for it can be simple like being grateful for running water to shower or waking up in the morning. It's up to you – just find some down time for you.

Weeks 2 to 6 - On repeat. See if any of these have become a part of your life and how you feel.

U is for UNDIVIDED.

High value men have strong focus and commitment to a singular goal or purpose. The key word is focus. When it comes to meeting people whether it be on dates, at work meetings or out socially, these men pay undivided attention to the person in front of them, are showing they respect other peoples' time.

Your takeaway from this: Don't be the guy they call Swiv. Swiv is someone who has trouble staying focused or maintaining eye contact with others.

Your head should not be constantly spinning around like a swivel chair every time someone walks past or moves in the background. Look grounded. Look focused. Look like you are present. Keep your head and neck still! Especially if you are on a date - it screams insecurity and low value if you leer or take sneaky glances at other women.

I is for INTELLIGENT

High value men are EQ and IQ masters in touch with their own emotions. If this is you, then you are driven, passionate, and have a personality worth noting. Highly intelligent, curious, and open-minded you become extremely attractive and hot. As hot as the burning footpaths exposed all day to the unforgiving Australian summer sun. You are a rare gem who knows how to engage in meaningful conversations, share ideas, who is big on personal growth.

Your takeaway from this: Google articles and read up on Social Emotional Learning (SEL) skills.

SEL tends to focus on students, but I believe it can also apply to adults. It strips behavioural standards back to the basics. It is the process of learning, applying, and directing a set of social, emotional, and related skills, attitudes, behaviours, and values. This includes thoughts, feelings, and actions that enable success.

R is for RAKISH

High value men have a rakish presence, meaning you are confident and carefree, generally disregarding social norms, like challenging the status quo. There is a sense of confidence and charm in his dashing, stylish, and slightly disreputable appearance. Self-confidence and daring attitude are often admirable traits.

Your takeaway from this: Appeal depends on several factors beyond just physical appearance which means everyone has a chance if they understand the other areas like behaviour also matters. Show respect for others. Be comfortable. Be confident, kind, and patient. Do not be afraid to laugh. Be yourself.

When getting ready, groom yourself and don't be afraid to dress to impress for you. Here's how it works.

Invest some time in your appearance. If you feel you have no clue on what clothes are in or out, take a moment to look at the clothing displays at the shopping mall. You can make a big difference by ironing and coordinating your clothes. Another alternative is to google department stores or well known menswear stores and browse through to get an idea of different styles. If you feel it, it's easier to own it and believe it.

T is for TASTE

High value men with impeccable taste know when to invest in quality and when to hold off. If this is you then you are confident, can recognise the difference between high-quality luxury items that last a lifetime and budget-friendly items that are still efficient even though it may not last as long. You steer clear of the lower quality goods designed for instant gratification as you know they do not last the distance compared to higher quality yet budget friendly taste comrades.

Your takeaway from this: Whether it be food, fashion, cars, art or women. You need to choose to invest wisely. Time is money and money is time.

The saying, 'Time only matters in jail', is wrong. Time and words are things you can never take back. You cannot turn back the clock. You cannot erase things from people's memories. So, try to behave and if you're online and feel someone is wasting your time, politely move on. Whatever you do, don't force the connection by saying you're deleting the app and asking for their phone number. It's an old trick that usually gets you an eyeroll.

O is for OBTAINABLE

High value men set the scene for being both obtainable yet attainable. Essentially, balancing attainable by being within reach to want more while being obtainable meaning available with future possibilities.

It's a very fine line but essentially, anyone approaching will be careful not to lose Mr Obtainable's desire or attention as his savvy ways give others enough give hope that he is available to potentially develop a meaningful relationship.

Your takeaway from this: It's all about balance. 'Hard to get' is an old school game that makes you look absent and a little flaky. On the other hand, being overly available will make you look lonely and desperate, like a thirsty camel on its 15th day without water.

Tip: Respond within the day with messages that contain more than just one word or an emoji. Keep it to less than three short sentences. Make sure your content is light and don't go into too much detail. Leave people wanting more.

R is for RELIABLE

High value men look as sleek as a Ferrari and are as reliable as a Toyota Corolla.

Your takeaway from this: So, you look like a Ferrari and you're reliable like a Toyota Corolla.

How?

1. Excellent deal at an affordable price: Like the guy everyone knows and likes, people appreciate you and you appreciate their time. You don't waste their time or yours.

2. Quality and quality control: You have higher standards than your rivals. Life engineering and design form the basis of your quality characteristics program. You are well put together and behave in a balanced manner. Consistency and stability are your best friends.

3. The safest option: Like the Corolla's sturdy construction, high-strength steel and stabilisers, you are trustworthy and safe. People know that if you say you will be there, you will be there. You do what you say.

4. Mileage and longevity: Compared to the average guy, you have better mileage and use fewer gallons of fuel - making you efficient. You don't drain people's energy by begging for attention, playing games, or overwhelming then by sending machine gun style text. messages. You respect people's time.

5. Excellent customer service: You listen. You are responsive. You are connected. You are polite. You are nice.

G is for GENUINE

High value men are authentic and sincere. They have the trust and respect of others. You give freely to others whether it be your time, resources, thoughts from the heart without expecting anything back.

Your takeaway from this: You cannot fake genuineness and sincerity. This is not a *fake it until you make it* thing. If you want to work in this area,

I'd recommend heading to the Mind Tools website and looking at the articles under personal branding. In particular, the article, *Authenticity, How to be True to Yourself.*

A is for AUTONOMOUS

High value men are independent. If this is you then, you make decisions. You don't need numbers or a voting council. You do the job with or without anyone's help.

Takeaway from this: You are the Bear Grylls of freedom, decision making and independence. Like Man vs. Wild you enter hostile social, work or dating environments like a SAS trooper, survival expert and adventurer. Leaving minimal damage. When you meet someone special, remember to offer them the seat beside you and not behind you or in front of you.

In case you've become a little scarred from negative experiences and you're still connected to hurt and not letting people in, check out Jay Shetty's podcasts. The amazing guests on his podcast will inspire you to become happier, healthier, and more healed.

S is for SELF

High value men take care of themselves. Through self-care a healthy and balanced lifestyle is maintained. Physical and mental well-being is a priority. Through self-esteem, you have self-confidence and self-worth while unapologetically aiming for success. Through self-respect you have set healthy boundaries.

Takeaway from this: It's simple.

Look after yourself. Invest in yourself.

Do you keep a clean car?

Do you service your car?

Do you pay for car insurance?

You are the vehicle that will take you through the rest of your life here on Earth. Don't be cheap when investing in yourself.

Make your mind happy by doing things you enjoy. Do things that can help your body perform better. Access activities that build you up and make you feel confident e.g. mentoring, self-growth.

M is for MAKER

High value men are makers through their craft. They are skilled artisans and incredibly talented. They put in the extra mile to produce the highest quality. These Makers are Masters.

Takeaway from this: Find something you like and are good at and focus on it. Build on it. Just choose something productive that gives you a sense of contribution. A person with an interest are always interesting to chat with. It is also a great conversation starter.

SHOPPING BASKET CHECKLIST

Don't let this opportunity pass you by. Start enjoying the benefits of your high value men's club membership and always read the labels before placing it into your basket.

It's time to secure your membership at the high value men club and here is your shopping basket for it.

Secure - Know your worth. Invest in yourself. Use positive self-dialogue.

Quality - Balance. Get the recipe right. Schedule time for yourself.

Undivided - Don't be the guy they call, Swiv.

Intelligent - Everyone knows how to Google. Look up articles, read them and enjoy opening your mindset.

Rakish - Be comfortable. Be confident, kind, and patient. Be yourself.

Taste – Whether it's food, fashion, friends etc invest wisely. Time is money and money is time.

Obtainable – Balance. Keep your content simple. Leave people wanting more.

Reliable - Look like a Ferrari, be reliable like a Toyota Corolla.

Genuine - Check out the Mind Tools website for articles on authenticity.

Autonomous - Offer that person you like the seat beside you, not in front of you or behind you.

Self - Don't be cheap when investing in yourself and your future.

Maker – Remember, a person with an interest is more interesting.

Breathe

Inhale

Exhale

Repeat

STEP 3: STAY IN YOUR LANE

To prevent social chaos, horses need to stay on their course just like swimmers need to stay in their lane.

Do dating apps and your local swimming pool have more in common than you think? Yes, they do!

ACCESS – SWIMMING POOL

Local swimming pools are the community's aquatic melting pot where everyone is welcome. This is no matter age, gender, sexuality, ethnicity, religion, sporting team or Spotify playlist.

Local swimming pools are required by law to maintain a level of disinfectant in the pool when operating for public health safety. However, not all organisms are killed by the disinfectants used in pools which may lead to nasties such as running to the loo every five seconds.

ACCESS – ONLINE DATING

One of the main advantages of dating apps is access to a large pool of potential suitors. But one must balance the old chestnut of quantity versus quality.

While you have the quantity, you face the risk of crossing virtual paths with those who falsify their profiles or intentions. This is like sticking the bull logo you normally see on a Lamborghini on the bonnet of a kit car - luxury imposter.

CONCEPT – SWIMMING POOL

These designated swimming spaces are provided for all types of swimmers according to their abilities. From recreational swimmers to professional athletes.

It is believed that there are over 1,000 public swimming pools in Australia, ranging from small community pools to large Olympic-sized pools.

- Swimming pools are designed for public safety.
- Swimming pools are intended to enhance swimmers' experiences.

- Swimming pools provide aquatic structure.
- Swimming pools foster social interaction among strangers.
- Swimming pools promote camaraderie and community.
- Swimming pools have rules and ask you to leave if you break them.

CONCEPT – ONLINE DATING

Globally, there are over 1,500 dating apps and websites with a market value projected to be over $9.2 billion.

- Dating apps have safety features.
- Dating apps are tailored to enhance the user's experience.
- Dating apps provide a well-structured platform for online dating.
- Dating apps can filter results based on desired criteria.
- Dating apps have community rules, and you can be banned with a few clicks.

- Dating apps allow users to send text messages, video calls, and voice calls and search for potential matches based on their location.
- Depending on which dating app you are using, dating apps can suggest potential matches based on common interests, desires, music taste or even their height, religion, nationality and physique.

LANES – SWIMMING POOL

Swimming pools have lanes that are designed to maintain world peace or at least order at the local swimming pool.

- Swimming pools have lanes that make up a peaceful symphony for those who enjoy swimming.
- Swimming pools have lanes to specify a swimmer's ability and speed.
- Swimming pool have lanes to function like town sheriffs without being in the same room.
- Swimming pool have lanes for swimmers to abide by with unspoken rules.

In most cases, swimming pools are divided into four lanes:

1. Fast lane

2. Medium lane

3. Slow lane

4. Recreation lane

LANES – ONLINE DATING

- Dating apps are designed to connect people whether they are looking for romance, friendship, or something casual.
- Dating apps are the most common way to meet new people in Australia.
- Dating apps provide a platform for users to connect with potential matches based on what they have put on their profile. In addition, they provide compatibility based on the app's algorithm.
- Through dating apps, users can meet people outside of their immediate social circle, state, and even country of origin.

In most cases, how you use a dating app can be divided into four categories:

1. Commitment

2. Connection

3. Recovery

4. Consensual

FAST LANE – COMMITMENT

Whether it be swimming in the fast lane or seeking a commitment online, these people are all about investment and intention.

FAST LANE – COMMITMENT – SWIMMING POOL

Moving in the fast lane.

- Swimmers in the fast lane have endurance, maintain high speeds, and are consistent.
- Swimmers in the fast lane have relatively high pool experience and confidence in their ability.

- Swimmers in the fast lane can be anything from professional athletes who are training for their next competition to individuals who are trying to maintain peak physical fitness levels.
- Swimmers in the fast lane work hard to maintain their performance.
- Swimmers in the fast lane tend to be committed and like long-term results.

FAST LANE – COMMITMENT – ONLINE DATING

Open to love.

- These virtual committed types pick specific apps and swipe with a purpose.
- These virtual committed types carefully read their prospective date's profile to understand what makes them tick.
- These virtual committed types look at their prospective dates' photos to work out if there is an attraction.
- These virtual committed types look at their prospective date's geographical location or distance to determine what is too far to pursue.

- These virtual committed types take time to look for a potential future with a partner and take responsibility for commitment.

MEDIUM LANE - CONNECTION

Whether it be swimming in the medium lane or seeking a connection online, these people balance managing curiosity and comfort. Not too hot and not too cold, just a little on the chill side.

MEDIUM LANE - CONNECTION - SWIMMING POOL

Pacing in the medium lane.

- An atmosphere of calm can be created by pacing in the middle lane.
- The medium lane allows swimmers to balance speed and comfort.
- The medium lane allows swimmers to maintain a comfortable pace and push themselves if they wish.
- Swimmers in the medium lane have moderate skills and endurance but may want to improve

stamina and speed without the intensity of the fast lane.

- Swimming in the medium lane is manageable and versatile. It is possible to train more and move up to the fast lane if interested in doing so.

MEDIUM LANE - CONNECTION - ONLINE DATING

Curious connections.

- Dating with an open mind and seeing if there's a connection.
- These virtual types test the waters in the online jungle to see if there are any connections out there.
- These virtual types are not exactly sure what they want, so don't tend to get too caught up on the destination.
- In the virtual world, these people take time to explore and are very curious about what's going on.

SLOW LANE – RECOVERY

Whether it be swimming in the slow lane or recovering in love rehab, this is all about recovery or rest.

SLOW LANE - RECOVERY - SWIMMING POOL

Recuperating in the slow lane.

- The slow lane is intended for beginners or those who prefer a slower pace.
- The slow lane is like an aquatic cushion for swimmers learning the waters or building confidence.
- Swimmers can improve their technique in the slow lane without feeling pressure from faster competitors.
- It is also beneficial to swim slowly after an intense workout to cool off.
- Besides providing shade and rest, the slow lane is also a convenient place to escape the heat.

SLOW LANE - RECOVERY - ONLINE DATING

Addressing issues and cleaning up the mess.

- Simple way to put it, the slow lane is the lane you recover in. It is the rehab of the love jungle.
- If you are recovering from a heartbreak, any dating let alone online dating can be difficult. If this is you, it's critical to give yourself time and space to heal before trying again.
- The most helpful advice I will offer you is this – delete the apps. Take care of yourself, hang out with people you know and trust, do things that bring you joy, exercise, eat healthy, sleep. It is all about self-care.
- The online jungle is unforgiving, and I'd suggest returning once you have replenished and recovered.

RECREATIONAL LANE- CONSENSUAL

Whether it be frolicking and splashing about in the recreational lane or seeking consensual hook ups online, these people are all about not committing or learning about swim strokes or online matches.

RECREATIONAL LANE- CONSENSUAL - LOCAL POOL

This lane is often located at the opposite end to the fast lane.

- The recreational lane is mostly reserved for people who do not wish to swim laps in the other lanes.
- There is a recreational lane for those who want to float, play water games, and do other aquatic activities.
- The recreational lane is usually located far away from the fast lane.
- Signs clearly indicate the area should be used only for recreational purposes.
- The recreational lane is predominately occupied by people who just want to get wet.

RECREATIONAL LANE- CONSENSUAL - ONLINE DATING

- No name or number required.

- The most accurate way to describe this is that they are not looking to date but more than just wanting to have a quick hook-up.
- Possibly accesses apps that only cover the faces of people rather than other parts of the body.

Dating apps/sites seem to be the most common way to meet new people. In Australia, it was estimated that over 3.2 million people using dating apps/sites.

Here are a few notable sites best suited for daters who are in the fast or medium lanes.

Bumble: A very popular dating apps/site. There is a strong emphasis on quality connections over hook-ups. After matching, Bumble requires women to message first. There is a free version with plenty of features. If you like women who make the first move, you'll love this app/site.

Coffee Meets Bagel: Keep things simple. User-friendly dating apps/sites. To save time and avoid overload, it limits the number of matches you get each day. There is a seven-day window in which you can contact your match. There is a free version. Those looking for a no-pressure dating site, or apps will love it.

eHarmony: A psychological profile is used as the basis for the matching. A great advantage if you're seeking love. Creating stronger relationships and marriages has always been the goal of the website. There is a free version. Filter by age to instantly narrow down the results. An excellent site if you're looking for love.

Elite Singles: Many single professionals use the site to find a partner. Many of them are over the age of 30. If you are ambitious, this is worth a try. You have high standards as a mature dater. In-depth profiles with a professional membership base.

Hinge: Makes the app/site more attractive to users and encourages them to delete it. Finds potential matches using intelligent algorithms and locations based on advanced preferences. There is a free version. There is a greater emphasis on relationships than hookups. The app/site is for you if you prefer conversations instead of swiping left or right.

Match: Match is a long-standing company for those looking for long-term relationships and who are family-minded, Match is fabulous. There is a rapid growth in the over-50 segment. There is a free version. Most members are over 30, lots of potential matches and detailed profiles.

Silver Singles: Over 20,000 new members per month in Australia and New Zealand. There are more than a third of members over the age of 50. It matches people based on their compatibility. There is a free version. Your best matches are sent to you every day. If you are looking for a 50+ match of good quality, this is the place to go.

Zoosk: You won't have to spend time looking at many unsuitable matches thanks to behavioural matchmaking technology. It has 38 million members worldwide. The Profile Carousel displays the profiles of people who are interested in meeting you. There is a free version. There are millions of members on the app/site in Australia, so it is likely to appeal to you.

There are also the following app/sites to name a few more Aussie Mingle, Badoo, Christian Dating Australia, Happn, OkCupid, Plenty of Fish, RSVP and Tinder

There are also apps/sites for recreational lane peeps seeking hook-ups or something more casual than a pair of sandals.

Adult Friend Finder: A racy dating app/site for adults who want to hang out engage with or without strings attached. The majority create accounts to flirt or hook up anonymously. This site once listed as has one of the largest online sex and swinger communities online. There is a free version. This site/app is your if you're looking for anonymous hook-ups.

Passion: It's like a toned-down version of Adult Friend Finder. This app/site is different from other hookup apps/sites in that it aims to create a community for its members. Creating a blog and writing about your interests is an option. There is a free version. Word has it that you'll love this if you're a mature dater into hook-ups or deep connections in a safe environment.

Most annoying things reported on the more casual apps/sites are explicit nudity and annoying ads may put off some people and lots of fake profiles.

Generally speaking, while apps are accessible, there are a few things that may not appeal to everyone:

- Can be pricey if you want all features
- Some users may have a difficult time matching due to the various ager demographic on apps/sites
- Can be expensive, free versions have limited features

- Sometimes you must pay to view match photos
- Expensive premium features, matches sourced from Facebook friends of friends
- Profiles are not as detailed as other apps/site
- Lots of upselling
- Long questionnaires at sign up
- Compatibility tests can take time
- Ads on sites

YOUR POST SWIM STRETCH

Ultimately, swimming pool lanes are much more than coloured lines. If you are swimming in the pool, make sure you choose the right lane for your skill level. By doing so, you will be able to maximize your swimming experience, while also ensuring the peace in the aquatic community.

When it comes to finding the right person (regardless of what you want), it's imperative to be open and honest about what you're seeking.

Don't put on your profile that you're looking for a relationship if you're looking to hook up. Rather put - I'm looking for something casual or NSA aka No Strings Attached.

If you smoke, don't pretend you don't on your profile - you can't mask the smoky tobacco smell.

Don't say you want kids on your profile if you don't.

In conclusion, swimming pool lanes are more than just coloured lines on the pool floor and dating apps are more than an icon on my phone... SIMPLE!

Vibe with your tribe!

STEP 4: PROFILE PITCH POWER

Poor profile quality is like being a rudderless ship in the dating app ocean.

In this digital age, profile photos have become an essential in this digital age, profiles have become an essential part of your online dating app presence. Why? Your profile consists of two main arenas... what you look like and what you are like. Whether you like it or not, your profile content serves as the first impression you make by creating an online presence. It gives the reader, swiper, and potential match more of who you are and whether you are worth investing in.

Here, we will explore the importance of dating app profiles and what unintentional messages you are sending through your photos and bio content. But before we say what to do here's what to avoid or what your profile might project.

PHOTOS

Let's start with photos. Does a photo really define a man? According to the book, *The Single Mother Trying Not to*

*F*ck Up Life (Mel W, 2019)*, it may not make the man, but it certainly makes an impression on the ladies or sends their imaginations down all sorts of paths.

A successful dating profile should include quality photos, positive points, and variety. By simply looking at photos alone, you can interpret or misinterpret a dating app profile in many ways. This 'harmless' rookie error can almost guarantee a missed match, or the dreaded swipe left. Check out how your online efforts can be misinterpreted by your profile viewers.

Do you sit down in every picture? There is a risk of appearing vertically challenged or even lying about your height on your profile (this is common amongst men) - try and mix it up just a bit. Make sure to include an accurate height in your profile.

Are you surrounded by scantily clad women in every photo? There's a chance you are David Copperfield trying to create the illusion that you're hotter than Brad Pitt or overcompensating for something else. Consider your audience and the type of people you are trying to attract.

Are you wearing a cap, hat, or beanie in every picture? Wearing a hat can also be a sign of laziness or having bad hair days constantly. Why? It takes little effort to don a hat rather than tending to your hair. If you are constantly covering your head due to going bald, hiding baldness whether it be due to heredity reasons, hormonal changes, or medical conditions. Take that hat off and let the bald dome shine with pride!

Do all your pictures have cluttered mess in the background, under the bed, on shelves? For some profile viewers may be thinking, I bet he's bloody lazy. Probably never changes his sheets. Leaves dirty plates in the sink without rinsing. Turns his underwear inside out to get an extra day's wear and avoid laundry! Probably doesn't manscape yet and expects women to resemble a Sphynx with a thin eyebrow down there. Harsh but possible. On dating apps, people are the judge, the jury and the executioner of your first impression.

Are all your pictures at the gym shirtless with bulging muscles? Most people assume they will receive an uninvited picture of a woodpecker! Why? This type of profiler 9 times of 10 will randomly strike with the wood pic more than once. If this is you.... consider changing your approach or use hookup apps.

Are you hiding your face? Most would conclude the person is married or is a well-known convicted sex offender! Most likely to call Crime Stoppers or Cheaters than your number.

Are all your photos blurry? Blurry photos scream cheap phone, cheap person who takes you to Costco for dinner. If you download the dating app, complete an account... clear photos are the easy part.

Do you only have group pictures, and everyone is hot except one? Ahhhh be careful that this is not the boy band theory. The theory is that every boy band needs one guy who attracts fans who can relate to him. Average looking Joe. Also remember you might receive a message asking to meet one of your friends in the photo.

Are you posing on the top of a mountain shirtless or doing an aerial skiing shot or on some insanely fast vessel? A testosterone fragrance in human form. It screams, I'm so full of testosterone fragrance that comes in a deodorant can labelled, "Me Tarzan. You Jane." Some love it, some run and sprint from it. Consider one photo if you must but five can be a bit much.

Are you holding or kissing a fish? STOP!! Do not upload that photo! I repeat, STOP! Do not upload that photo!!

HERE ARE SOME SIMPLE TIPS TO TAKE YOUR ONLINE EXPERIENCE TO THE NEXT LEVEL.

High-quality images

Avoid pixelated or grainy pictures as they project a lack of attention to detail. Make sure your photos are presentable, clear and not over filtered. Snapchat character filters aren't a great look for anyone old enough to have a tax file or social security number. Do not use blurry or out of focus photos or ones with half of your head chopped off. Ensure your profile photo is clear, well-lit, and in focus.

Choose recent photos

Using an outdated photo may lead to confusion and disappointment when meeting in person. It's critical to select a profile photo that accurately represents your current appearance.

Smile with eye contact

A genuine smile can go a long way to creating a positive impression. Additionally, making eye contact with the camera conveys confidence and approachability.

Check the background

Your profile photo background should be simple and uncluttered, drawing attention to you rather than distractions. A plain backdrop or blurred background can work well.

Dress appropriately

Watch the length of your shirt. If it's too short, it's not flattering. Having your lower tummy exposed under an ill-fitting shirt is as bad as having dirty nails. Choose clothing that aligns with your personal style. Ensure your clothing is stainless, fits well and flatters your body.

Be mindful of photos with family &/or with kids

Some photos are nice, but your family or kids may not want to be on your dating app profile. Seeing profiles full of father of the year photos can be overwhelming for a potential suitor. Taking pictures with your kids are not necessary. Just tell them you're a father if you want to.

Make an effort at editing

Avoid photos where you scribble someone's face out or cover it with an emoji. Looks messy, distracting and lowers your profile's quality. Crop the person from the photo. Every phone has a camera with built in editing tools.

Limit group photos

Messy drunken photos will make you look immature and sloppy. Be careful. Sometimes women prefer to look at the person you are standing next to instead of you. Too many and people get lost and confused trying to figure out which one is you. This is almost swiping left worthy as the effort required to figure out which one is you is time-consuming. Just one or two clear group photos if you must.

Cap the number of obvious selfies

Unless you're hotter than the summer sun, avoid silly faces with crossed eyes. Numerous selfies in the same outfit and similar poses or multiple mirror selfies are not an appealing look and are quite boring and cringeworthy.

Mix it up. Variety is the visual spice. Even better use your phone's camera timer, stand back so it doesn't look like a selfie!

Work or event pics are not necessary

Just be aware your colleagues may be mortified to be in a photo on a dating app. Also, do you really want your company's name exposed? There would be nothing more frightening than a call to your work from a connection not happy to be disconnected.

BIO CONTENT

Research suggests that first impressions are formed within seconds, and profile photos play a significant role in this process as people form judgments based on visual cues. The other aspect that is equally important is that your profile, also known as your bio, is written in a way that captures attention to leave a lasting impression in this online jungle.

Okay, so here are some tips....

Put your best foot forward in your profile

Don't be afraid to fill out all the dating app fields.

The app's algorithm also works better when you fill out all fields so that it can suggest better matches based on the detailed information you provide. Plus, an engaging bio is crucial because it provides a deeper insight into who you are beyond just your appearance. It helps potential matches get your vibe and see if you could both belong to the same tribe. Check for typos and spelling errors.

Honesty is always the best policy. Be honest about your age, height, religion, desire for children, drinking or smoking habits. Here's the truth: if you're 5'8" and you say you're at least 6'0", you better wear concealed stilts on your first date. Prince was the only man I knew of who could carry off wearing high heeled boots.

Your intro? Positive thinking is the key. Lighten up. Ensure that it is easy to read. Keep your writing away from things you don't like about women or what you don't want from them. No one wants to read a country and western song.

Use prompted questions. Be bold! Get creative! Don't be too serious. You can use a song or movie as an example.

Keep it simple and focus on the positives. Take advantage of the prompted questions.

Avoid a Santa's wish list. When you list what you are looking for in your bio in a person. Be warned; to demand she have qualities on your wish list, it is assumed that you must have the same qualities and then some.

Take it easy. There is no need to write about your financial status. It comes across as desperate and you don't get interest online. Flex later if you must.

Choose your words wisely. When you describe yourself as baggage free it can imply that potential suitors with histories are not invited to connect, and you have effectively reduced your market!

Be careful about your projection.

By writing about seeking someone who doesn't lie and is trustworthy and loyal, you may come across as someone with trust issues and hard work.

Those who are parents don't need to write in their bios that their children are the most important people in their lives. This is a given and comes across as tacky and uninspiring.

CATCH OF THE DAY TAKEAWAY

So, to round off let me give you an analogy of why having a quality dating app profile is so crucial. Think of yourself as your own brand, marketing and customer service manager.

If you position yourself as someone of quality, who is articulate and well put together then it will be like fishing on a trawler with a team of fishermen out at sea capturing the most amazing amount of incredibly attractive looking and intelligent fish.

If you make reasonable effort, then it is possible that trawler will turn into a shitty little dinghy with one lonely fisherman changing bait every five seconds trying to catch a decent looking and coherent fish.

If you barely make any effort, it is possible the dinghy will become a pool scooper scraping up leaves and weeds at the bottom of the pool.

If you make zero effort or portray yourself as a bit of a social jerk, then it is possible you are more like a fishbowl scooper desperately trying to catch the micro parasites feeding off the side of fishbowl scum.

Oh yes… the latest craze I have seen is for men over a certain age taking dressing room mirror selfies… with tags on the clothes. If this is, you… please close my book, hold it closed with one hand and slap yourself!!

Remember, your profile is an opportunity to showcase your personality, qualities, visual pleasantness and approachability, so make it count!

Oh, and another thing, about to travel? Set your dating app to travel mode to start connecting with potential suitors before you arrive at your destination.

*Don't agonise when you
choose to economise.*

STEP 5: LITERACY IN
THE ONLINE JUNGLE

*Virtual literacy can be the difference between becoming
a statue or a pigeon.
In other words, the shitter or the shat upon.*

Virtual literacy can take you a long way in the online jungle. It can be the difference between becoming a statue or a pigeon. In other words, the shitter or the shatter.

In today's digital age, understanding virtual and textual spaces is crucial when navigating the online jungle full of exotic fruit, fruit bats and bat droppings.

If you follow psychologist Albert Mehrabian's 7-38-55 rule, which deals with emotion communication you might be on the backfoot. He proposed in his book Silent Messages (1971) is that your words communicate 7%, your tone 38%, and your body language 55% which is part of the challenge of reading in the virtual room through messages as tone and language are absent which equates to 93% of emotional communication is missing.

Although instant messaging is convenient and flexible, it lacks the body language, facial expressions, and tone of voice that convey emotion and intent better than face-to-face communication. So how does this work if you rely on 7% emotional communication to make a connection?

You might think it is easier to climb Mount Everest in a pair of crocs and a 100kg backpack. Simple: Knowing how trees sway in the online jungle will save you time with people who are only looking for validation or who aren't that interested.

Call this a boot camp session with Survivor's, *Eye of the Tiger* blasting for motivation. Okay, so tic-tac-toe here we go....

YOUR FIRST MESSAGE

HERO: Keep your messages light, simple and positive. Look for something you have in common with them to open a dialogue online, for example what they have written on their profile or what they have posted online. Let's go beyond an emoji or just one word and embrace something a little more meaningful.

ZERO: There's a tendency among people to tell people they're financially secure in hopes of attracting ladies or getting more jungle time. Please don't send a long message outlining your CV and stating your financial security. Please don't. That's just not cool and won't attract or keep the right people. This is a dating app not a letter to your loan officer. It scares away high value people and smells desperate. Don't use long winded copied and pasted messages. Rookies use templates.

RESPONDING TO THEIR FIRST MESSAGE

YAY: It would be ideal if you could respond on the day to send a vibe of interest. Read their message and respond with something that is a reply to their first message, then ask a question. Open the lines of communication.

NAY: In the case of responding within seconds, it might seem as if there are little or no options to choose from. Having deliberately waited for days could be viewed as a sign that you are not interested in starting a connection. Don't use long winded copied and pasted messages. Rookies use templates and they are exhausting for the audience.

SARCASM

MMM: Keep your sarcasm to a minimum until you know each other well enough to avoid offending each other. If you're going to use sarcasm, ask yourself, what are you trying to say? If your communication too sarcastic, you will probably look nasty or a little misogynistic. Some people are quite sensitive, and you do not know what their story is. If you use heavy sarcasm to joke or tease someone, don't confuse it with light-hearted teasing.

MESSAGES IN GENERAL

WOO: In a way, chatting online is the same thing as chatting with someone you don't know in a bar or social setting - you approach them with the intention of getting to know them better. Don't take it too seriously and keep it light-hearted. Honesty and openness are good, but not too much. You're still online, so stay in the square since you're not in their circle. Do not pressure the other person. Respect their boundaries. Enjoy the conversation and have fun!

NOO: Drowning them with messages like a machine gun and expecting them to respond to each one is too stressful and demanding. Let's think about tennis for a moment.

Your opponent doesn't get a chance to respond if you hit multiple balls at them at once. Wait for them to hit the ball back before you return it again. You should avoid oversharing your relationship history, which is another major boo boo. Talking about a past relationship in the early days of messaging can be annoying. Focus on the present.

PHOTOS

DEFINITELY: It's fine if you wish to send each other photos - if you both agree to do so. Be respectful of the other person's privacy and don't share photos without their permission. Make sure you have a good understanding of what you are exchanging, so it's always a pleasant surprise as opposed to unexpectedly receiving a pecker pic!

DEFINITELY NOT: It is not appropriate to share uninvited pictures of your pecker. It's harassment. Don't send pecker pics and respect their boundaries. Additionally, beware of selfie tombs, where you send tons of photos of yourself spanning across the years in one day. It is hideously overwhelming.

CORRECTNESS

MMM: Please do not tell them that they should fix any typos or errors in their profiles. Just relax. Ask yourself, why would you need to point out superficial errors about someone you want to connect with? Correcting someone's content on their profile serves little purpose and makes you appear uptight, or you have the potential to be controlling or domineering.

READ THE ROOM

OH YEAH: Like for like. If you keep messaging the same person without receiving a response, take a breather - move on. In other words, respond or unmatch them if they return. If they choose to respond, give them another chance. If not, it's time to move on. The ball is in your court.

OH NO: The first thing you need to remember is that politeness is not the same as interest. You might get sporadic inconsistent responses, which could mean that the person is polite, but isn't interested enough in you to invest in consistency.

SOCIAL MEDIA

OK: If you would like to follow them on their social media accounts, ask them if you can do so. Seeing who they follow will give you an idea of who and what they like, who and what they're interested in, and so on.

CREEPY: Sneaking uninvited photos of your pecker into their DMs without their permission will have them thinking the same offending sex pest has done it again! There most likely half a million Instagram users who have received that pecker photo as well! If you like every previous post in order to get their attention, you look too eager!

VOICE MESSAGES

BOOM: Make sure you mix up the types of texts you send, voice recordings you make, and video calls. It is always fun to have variety in your life.

TOMB: An excessive number of hyper-animated recordings can irritate the recipient and make it harder for him or her to respond to your message. Shorter recordings are easier to understand and keep the conversation flowing. But not too many.

Here's a prime example: you connect with a woman.
You message her on the app using the first 4 voice messages that are as high-energy as a motivational speaker. The connection fizzles fast and you are now randomly unmatched. Alone. No more communication channels.

Why?

Because it got too intense too fast. Too much pressure too soon. The recipient would probably didn't have the energy to send multiple voice message responses sounding like salespeople on the shopping network channel.

TRYING TO TEASE

HMMM: Sometimes people find it funny to tease others with messages such as:
- You think you're sooooo talented.
- Let me guess you're single because you choose to be.
- What do you think of your profile? Is it funny or good enough to attract my attention?
- You are leading us all on with your profile.

- I only like hot intelligent women. Do you think you're the one?

Most recipients would not find this funny at all. In addition to being annoying, it can sometimes scream at them to run as fast as they can! If you do this and your very own profile is uninspiring and hideously monotonous, it's even worse.

When the walls of your house are as thin as sliced cheese, there's no point throwing dating profile stones! This is as cheap as wearing a second-hand stained polyester suit and as nasty as the stench from wearing it in the middle of a summer heat wave!

SELF-DEPRECATING HUMOUR

HMMM: It's okay to laugh at yourself sometimes, but don't let it degrade you to the point that you're unattractive. You can boost your confidence by laughing at yourself, but don't become too self-deprecating.

TODAY'S LESSON

ABC is like 123. To round this up – there are no complicated rules. It's quite simple. Strip it back.

A. Make sure you don't type anything you wouldn't say in person. Don't say anything that you wouldn't do yourself.

B. Sometimes, silence is their response.

C. Strike a balance between being humble, not taking yourself too seriously, and playing nicely!

*Don't procrastinate,
instead marinate.*

STEP 6: THE FOUR FLAGS

Therapist: You saw the red flags though, right?

Patient: Yes, but I thought it was a carnival!

Let's move ahead to our next step now that the messages are coming in.

Let's discuss flags. Flags represent nations, states, or organisations. They identify groups of people and brings them together. It represents many things.

For this step, we will select four flags that represent a person's characteristics, personality, behaviours and social style.

These flags will help you identify whether to proceed with confidence with the connection, proceed with caution with the connection, end the connection instantly or close the connection as you're on the wrong data plan.

To assess our flags, we'll use the RAG system. It's also known as the traffic light approach using Red, Amber, and Green. It's great for tracking, identifying, and evaluating threats and areas that need attention. A fourth flag, the checkered flag has been added. This step is about showing you what to look for and what to run from.

GREEN FLAGS

The situation is neither critical nor urgent. It seems that things are going well with no concerns being raised. No guesswork, no games, and no overthinking. Let's say you've been chatting and connected with someone online and you're ready to meet.

A green flag worthy person will be quite secure within themselves. The person doesn't have to be super confident, but they should carry themselves with enough confidence to be emotionally intelligent. Being respectful of others and being able to compromise is essential.

- They have a strong sense of boundaries
- Communicate healthily
- They celebrate your achievements with you
- You support and encourage each other's goals
- Conflict is dealt with in a healthy and constructive way
- They bring out your green flags

- When they make plans, you are considered
- You both have similar beliefs, values and goals
- Honesty and respect cannot be overstated
- A supportive attitude
- There's a sense of comfort and safety between you
- Takes responsibility for self-improvement
- They are consistent and reliable
- Emotionally available
- It's easy for them to get along with people
- When you talk, they listen

They haven't asked you about your ex, your bad breakups, or your salary then that's a green flag. On the other hand, if you ask about these, stop.

To put it simply, if you want to attract green flags, make sure you too can be considered a green flag.

AMBER FLAGS

Critical but not urgent. There's a problem, but it can be fixed. This situation should be monitored, reviewed and assessed before any decisions are made. It's important to take decisive action as soon as possible.

- There is a blurring of boundaries
- Communication is inconsistent
- They're not overly interested in talking about your wins and goals
- Avoids dealing with conflicts or brushes issues to the side
- You're not usually considered when planning, sort of an afterthought
- Although you're on a similar page with your beliefs, they differ
- There's a sense of comfort and safety between you
- You don't really have many common interests
- Self-awareness could be improved with some work
- You're on their mind but only when they're bored.
- They confuse being assertive with just trying to do the opposite of most things
- When you talk, they're not overly focused

They ask you random questions about your ex, your past lovers. Feeling judged, uncomfortable or interrogated? Tell them this and if they persist, shut it down and walk away.

They hint at how much money you earn. They talk about their debt very early on in the connection. Politely change the subject or tell them it's not ideal to talk about finances. If they persist, end the conversation and consider this upgraded in risk status to red flag!

Individually, some of these qualities aren't deal breakers and can be addressed with mature conversation, but if there are a lot of them, this should be a deal breaker.

RED FLAGS

It is likely that the connection will suffer serious damage if nothing is done to fix the problem as soon as possible. There's a huge potential for disruption. Take immediate action. Walk away! Get on your scooter and ride out of there. Actually… just run.

- Ignoring your boundaries and not respecting them
- Having a critical attitude towards friends and family members
- They speak poorly of their ex-partners regularly
- An absence of trust is a major problem
- Abuse of substances
- Behaviours that are abusive

- It gets too serious too soon
- The love bombing phenomenon
- A tendency to obsess over social media
- Avoidance of serious emotional connection
- Feeling insecure in the connection and manipulating and controlling
- The gaslighting technique
- The lack of communication has been a problem
- They tell you that all their exes were crazy people
- Maintaining a high degree of secrecy
- Blame others
- Extreme emotional reactions and angry outbursts
- Irresponsible, immature, and unpredictable
- Self-centredness and narcissism
- They guilt-trip you constantly
- They seek too much attention

THE FINISH LINE: WAVING THE CHECKERED FLAG

Checkered flag signals the end of the race. When the winner crosses the finish line, they're hoisted. This is the flag waved when the race is officially over. So, here are a few examples of when to wave the checkered flag.

A connection has been made and they have lots of green flags. Do you want to move forward to the first date or another date? Get out there and wave this flag because you are ready to proceed to the next level of connection with the person you are talking to. This flag is a symbol of hope and optimism that things are going to work out.

You made a connection, but it fizzled. Now this wasn't due to red flags or too many amber flags. The connection just dropped out like the cheapest internet package on a cruise ship. Nothing too drastic. Maybe you're just not into them or they're just not into you. It's classic when you're online that the contact is quite saturated and exciting at first, then it just goes flat. So, save your life data and wave the checkered flag.

You find a connection and you notice an amber flag or two. It's an excellent idea to see if these amber flags can be tolerated or worked through in the early days. Given it is relatively early, cut your losses and reinvest. Pay attention to your gut instincts. If something doesn't feel right, it's not worth investing in it. Move on and find something better. Be careful not to be seduced by loneliness or desperation into accepting something you wouldn't normally accept. If you ask yourself too often whether their amber flags are bad... you're probably right and it's time to wave the checkered flag.

Discovered red flags? Wave the checkered flag now! Run! Sprint! Crawl!

Keep going...

STEP 7: UNITING THE PAST
AND THE PRESENT

"Don't dress to kill, dress to survive."

"Sweatpants are a sign of defeat. You lost control of your life so you bought some sweatpants."

"Trendy is the last stage before tacky."

— Karl Lagerfeld

While Karl did not have online dating in mind with his wise advice, the principles can be applied.

"Don't dress to kill, dress to survive."

Find that balance in your dating app profile. Avoid oversaturating your profile with details about your past, present, and hopes for what your future partner will be like. You might end up looking cheesy or even worse... greasy. Don't smother the reader to death with words. This also applies to messaging on apps.

"Sweatpants are a sign of defeat. You lost control of your life so you bought some sweatpants."

How are you responding to messages or sending messages? Kill the emoji only response. It looks lazy. It's like you've been using the apps for so long and have been unsuccessful, so you have become a lacklustre texter. You'll lose the gig before it starts.

"Trendy is the last stage before tacky."

Okay, so I am going to come out and say this. It's not a good idea to wear skinny jeans or chinos over a certain age. Dad bods in skinny jeans can look weird. Look at Gru from Minions. Make sure your clothes complement your shape. You don't have to change your style for anyone, but don't risk losing points over something so simple.

"Don't count the days, make the days count."

"Often it isn't the mountains ahead that wear you out, it's the little pebble in your shoe."

"Float like a butterfly, sting like a bee. The hands can't hit what the eyes can't see."

— *Muhammad Ali*

In honour of one of the greatest heavyweight boxers of all time, Muhammed's words are as powerful as his hits. This my dear friend, is something you'll need to do in the dating app ring.

"Don't count the days, make the days count."

There's been a lot of texting/messaging. It's been weeks. She has your attention. You are both from the same city. You have asked to meet her several times. But she declines every time with an excuse. However, she still flirts with you online. If you have a romantic interest, my dear reader, I advise you to make your days count and walk away. If a woman really wants to meet you, she'll find a way.

"Often it isn't the mountains ahead that wear you out, it's the little pebble in your shoe."

Being single is better than being in an unfulfilling situation. You connect with someone online. They demand your immediate attention. If you don't answer right away, they get mad at you, throw a hissy fit or worse sulk.

Even though you see these signs, you don't get many quality matches, so you ignore the lack of respect. This person will exhaust you and probably make you feel guilty, and you'll feel the little pebble in your shoe sucking the life out of you and you'll be back alone with one hand reaching for the happy tissues. Remember happy tissues are far better than sad tissues.

"Float like a butterfly, sting like a bee. The hands can't hit what the eyes can't see."

When interacting with someone online, always be kind. If they are rude, don't stoop to their level or lower your own standards. An example, some people online have a major flaw is that they like to brag about how hot their other matches are on the apps. If this happens to you….

DO NOT ENGAGE!

Keep your composure and unmatch with them. I'm hoping your quick action of setting a boundary will help the perp behave better in the future. You got your say by not having to say anything. Efficiency is key with your time. Far more powerful position to be in.

CHANGE THE FREQUENCY and CEASE all airtime.

"Before you embark on a journey of revenge, dig two graves."

"Life is really simple, but we insist on making it complicated."

"He who will not economize will have to agonize."

— Confucius

The ancient Chinese philosopher Confucius has shaped cultures and societies for centuries with his ideas. While he wasn't responsible for classic lines such as, be kind and rewind, from your Blockbuster video store or, don't be silly and wrap your willy, slogans used in school development classes.

Guess what? Confucianism has hit the online dating world in several ways, from wisdom and success to virtue and compassion.

"Before you embark on a journey of revenge, dig two graves."

You had a horrible breakup. You are angry. Don't want a relationship, just want to mess around on the apps and hook up with as many people as possible. Be honest and upfront that you are not in the market for a relationship. Talking like you're in the market looking for a relationship when you aren't isn't cool. Especially as you know the other person is looking for a relationship.

Don't sell them a fake designer bag. Karma will find you and slap you silly and so hard that you travel through atmospheric layers from the troposphere beyond the exosphere to the Edge of Outer Space known as the Karman line.

"He who will not economize will have to agonize."

You meet someone online. They are stunning. You notice some flaws. But they are sexy. They show some negative signs. But they are gorgeous. You know your friends will salivate. It will make you feel like you have a trophy to show off.

Some men just like to be next to someone who looks much better than their behaviour. Is this you? Happy to date the hot meanie? Make sure you respect yourself and don't settle for cheap champagne poured into an empty used Krug bottle.

"Life is really simple, but we insist on making it complicated."

Many people report that dating apps are exhausting and waste their time, and they are over the dead ends or the drama. Take a break from them. It's that simple.

Now for a little fun… here are a few other lines that may not be as inspirational or deep, but they are kind of funny. I will warn each one of you to use these with extreme caution. Now these could see you get a laugh, and you connect or blocked without a disconnection notice. The choice is yours….

All the good pick-up lines are taken but you aren't.

Are you a charger? Because I'm dying without you.

Are you a keyboard? Because you might just be my type.

Are you a Mariah Carey song? Because All I Want for Christmas Is You.

Are you a parking ticket? Because you've got 'Fine' written all over you

Are you Siri? Because you autocomplete me.

Aren't you worried about global warming? Because you're making it hot in here.

Do you have a map? Because I keep getting lost in your eyes

Do you have a mirror? Because I can see us together.

Do you have a name? Or can I call you mine?

Excuse me while I delete my dating apps.

Excuse me, but I think you dropped something: my jaw

I bet my number sounds nicer than yours. Wanna hear it?

I don't normally chase people but for you I'd put my crocs in sport mode.

I have a phone number; you have a phone number—think of the possibilities.

If you let me borrow a kiss, I promise I'll give it right back.

I'm lost. Can you give me directions to your heart?

I'm not currently an organ donor, but I'd love to give you my heart.

Is your name Google? Because you've got everything I'm searching for

Is your name Jimmy? Because I've Fallon for you.

Is your name Wi-Fi? Because I'm really feeling a connection

I've got all these forks and knives all I need is a little spoon.

My name is [your name] but you should hear my phone number.

This must be a museum because you're a work of art.

Well, here I am. What are your other two wishes?

You can delete the app now, I'm here.

You know, I'm terrible at flirting. How about you try to pick me up instead?

Your hand looks heavy, can I hold it for you?

Your lips look lonely. Would they like to meet mine?

*Don't force the sauce out
of the bottle.*

STEP 8: SOCIAL MEDIA HOUSEKEEPING

Life is like an onion. You peel it off one layer at a time, and sometimes you weep

We are going to talk about housekeeping. What do I mean by housekeeping? I'm talking about cleaning up your digital space. Deleting apps, you don't use anymore is a good start. Get rid of your old messages and emails. Get rid of any accounts you don't use.

Oh, and while I'm here, if you want to share social media details, check out who you're following. From what you like and who you follow, people get an idea of how they perceive or judge you.

You might be perceived to the person you're connected with that you're not that interested in a real connection because you follow a lot of half-naked travel influencers, or lingerie-wearing food influencers, or soft porn models.

Men can get themselves into trouble when they whisper sweet nothings to their object of desire while they validate their half-naked or totally naked social media models by liking every one of their posts. Keep in mind that when you follow each other, you can see what each other likes. I have seen this firsthand bring couples undone.

I'm not saying jump in and delete, I'm saying just be mindful that such things can paint a picture of you that is not entirely true. It's probably good to look at who they follow and their interests as well.

If they have a heavy presence on social media posting every second of their day and you're a very private person, set your boundaries on what you are comfortable being see on.

If you get some great shots on a date and want to post them on your social media, ask them if they're okay with it. If they're going to post your picture on a platform that goes out to the whole world, they should ask you too.

When do you ask them for their social media details? I'd wait for them to ask you.

If you can't wait, just remember being too eager to peek into someone's private affairs too soon might make them pull away since you'll come off as moving too fast.

Don't like all their past posts - you weren't even in their life, and it has a stench of desperation lingering. Stick to liking the present posts.

If you have just connected, do not comment on their posts. You may be booted off their account as their friends and family ask, 'Who is this Rando Brando commenting on your posts?

Make sure you respect boundaries like local councils do. They don't collect garbage outside of their local government area.

Don't say anything on social media you wouldn't say in person.

Don't tag them on reels or posts, it's too early. Further down the path is totally fine but in the very early stages go easy. You too run the risk of the advice I said not to do if you let them into your world online.

They then see your friends' and family members' names. If they tend to snoop, they could get jealous of happy photos of you with your friends or family members thinking they are an ex. This is a red flag!

You don't need to share your social media details if you're still trying to figure out if you'll be sleeping with one eye open or blissfully spooning.

Some people will feel more comfortable sharing only certain accounts rather than all of them. For example, they are happy to share their Instagram posts, but not their Facebook posts.

HOUSEKEEPING TIPS YOU

Never ever try these and disengage with anyone who does it to you.

- Sending unsolicited pics of your pecker. It's almost offensive that I have to tell people this - but a lot of people do it.
- Constantly spamming and bombarding their DMs
- Jealous of their posts and asking why they're with whom they're pictured.
- Sending DMs to people who ignore your texts and WhatsApp is one way to get blocked so fast you'll catch a cold.
- Contact people in their social media community to troll, skite, introduce yourself or stalk.

Flex! You got this!

STEP 9: YOU'RE READY – HERE'S THE SUMMARY

THEIR CODE AND YOUR BOUNDARIES

YOUR TAKEAWAY CONTAINER

Be aware that not everyone knows how to behave. Sometimes it is not about you. It's about them.

1. If it looks like a duck, behaves like a duck, and quacks like a duck, it's probably a duck. Don't ignore the situation, act.
2. Your boundaries are more significant than their codes. Staying is a choice and walking away is also a choice.
3. It is a bizarre jungle out there and you need to prepare for the worst while hoping for the best. Know when to hold 'em and when to fold 'em.

HIGH VALUE MEN

SHOPPING BASKET CHECKLIST

1. **S**ecure - Know your worth. Invest in yourself. Use positive self-dialogue.
2. **Q**uality - Balance. Get the recipe right. Schedule time for yourself
3. **U**ndivided - Don't be the guy they call, Swiv.
4. **I**ntelligent - Everyone knows how to Google. Look up articles or read them.
5. **R**akish - Be comfortable. Be confident, kind, and patient. Be yourself.
6. **T**aste - Invest wisely. Time is money and money is time.
7. **O**btainable - Keep your content simple. Leave people wanting more.
8. **R**eliable - Look like a Ferrari, be reliable like a Toyota Corolla.
9. **G**enuine - Check out the Mind Tools website for articles on authenticity.
10. **A**utonomous - Offer that person the seat beside you, not behind you.
11. **S**elf - Don't be cheap when investing in yourself and your future.

12. **Maker** - A person with an interest is more interesting.

STAY IN YOUR LANE

YOUR POST SWIM STRETCH

1. When it comes to finding the right person (regardless of what you want), it's imperative to be honest and open about what you're seeking.
2. Don't say you're seeking a relationship if you're looking to hook up. Rather put - I'm looking for something casual or NSA aka No Strings Attached.
3. If you smoke, don't pretend you don't on your profile - you can't mask the smokey tobacco smell.
4. Don't say you want kids on your profile if you don't.

PPP: PROFILE PITCH POWER

CATCH OF THE DAY TAKEAWAY

1. Having a quality dating app profile is crucial. You are your own brand, marketing and customer service manager.
2. If you position yourself as someone of quality, who is articulate and well put together then it will be like fishing on a trawler with a team of fishermen out at sea capturing the most amazing amount of incredibly attractive looking and intelligent fish.
3. If you make reasonable effort, then it is possible that trawler will turn into a shitty little dinghy with one lonely fisherman changing bait every five seconds trying to catch a decent looking and coherent fish.
4. If you barely make any effort, it is possible the dinghy will become a pool scooper scraping up leaves and weeds at the bottom of the pool.
5. If you make zero effort or portray yourself as a bit of a social jerk, then it is possible you are more like a fishbowl scooper desperately

trying to catch the micro parasites feeding off the side of fishbowl scum.

6. Remember, your profile is an opportunity to showcase your personality, professionalism, and approachability, so make it count!

LITERACY IN THE ONLINE JUNGLE

TODAY'S LESSON

ABC is like 123. To sum it up – there are no complicated rules. It's quite simple. Strip it back.

A. Make sure you don't type anything you wouldn't say in person. Don't say anything that you wouldn't do to yourself.
B. Sometimes, silence is their response.
C. Strike a balance between being humble, not taking yourself too seriously, and playing nicely!

THE FOUR FLAGS

THE FINISH LINE: WAVING THE CHECKERED FLAG

Checkered flags signal the end of the race. When the winner crosses the finish line, they're hoisted. This is the flag waved when the race is officially over. Examples of when to wave the checkered flag.

1. You made a connection, but it fizzled. Now this wasn't due to red flags or too many amber flags. The connection just dropped out like the cheapest internet package on a cruise ship. Nothing too drastic. So, save your life data and wave the checkered flag.

2. You find a connection and notice an amber flag or two. Pay attention to your gut instincts. If something doesn't feel right, it's not worth investing in it. Move on and find something better. Don't be seduced by loneliness or desperation into accepting something you wouldn't normally accept. If you ask yourself too often whether their

amber flags are bad... you're probably right and it's time to wave the checkered flag.

3. Discovered red flags? Wave the checkered flag now! Run! Sprint! Crawl!

THE PAST AND THE PRESENT UNITE

1. Find that balance in your dating app profile. Avoid oversaturating your profile with details.
2. Kill the emoji only response. It looks lazy. You'll lose the gig before it starts.
3. Make sure your clothes complement your shape. You don't have to change your style for anyone, but don't risk losing points over something so simple.
4. You have asked to meet her several times. She declines to meet always with an excuse. Make your days count and walk away. If a woman really wants to meet you, she'll find a way.
5. Being single is better than being in an unfulfilling situation. You'll feel the little pebble in your shoe sucking the life out of you and you'll be back alone with one hand reaching for the happy tissues. Remember happy tissues are far better than sad tissues.

6. Always be kind. If they are rude, don't stoop to their level or lower your own standards.

7. Keep your composure when unmatching with someone. You got your say by not saying anything. Efficiency is the key to making the most of your time. Far more powerful position to be in.

8. Be honest and upfront that you are not looking for a relationship. Talking like you're looking for a relationship when you aren't isn't cool. Don't sell them fake designer bags. Karma will find you and slap you silly.

9. Some men just like to be next to someone who looks better than their behaviour. Is this you? Happy to date the hot meanie? Make sure you respect yourself and don't settle for cheap champagne poured into a Krug bottle.

10. Finding dating apps exhausting and a waste of time? Take a break from them. It's that simple.

SOCIAL MEDIA HOUSEKEEPING

1. Don't like all their past posts. Stick to liking the present posts.
2. If you have just connected, do not comment on their posts.
3. Make sure you respect boundaries like local councils do.
4. Don't say anything on social media you wouldn't say in person.
5. Don't tag them on reels or posts, it's too early.
6. If they jealous of happy photos of you with your friends or family members thinking they are an ex. This is a red flag!
7. You don't need to share your social media details if you're still trying to figure out if you'll be sleeping with one eye open or blissfully spooning.

And there you have it my friends. It is time to put yourself out there. Thank you for sharing your time on this journey. If by chance you want more information you can always visit www.melwandco.com

"The successful
man will profit
from his mistakes
and try again in a
different way."

—Dale Carnegie